Butterfly

poems

Nader Qamhiyeh

To order additional copies of this book, contact:
Xlibris
1-888-795-4274
www.Xlibris.com
Orders@Xlibris.com
815117

When will you begin that long
journey into yourself -Rum-

PART ONE:
THE BUG

Larva

Breaking out of my comfort zone,
to venture through the unknown,
feeling intoxicated with glee:
observing,
sightseeing,
looking up;
noticing powder-blue skies
with folding hearts—
and castles turning to smiling faces—
a yellow orb shines between.

"Wow! What's that?"

Butterfly

Sol! giving life,
and nutrient to other beings.

Butterfly

Winged animals sing,
perched on parchment wood,
etching in nature,
and striking curious poses.

Smaller critters—
red and black,
pulling and pushing—
constructing little forts.
There are other winged ones,
vibrant in color—
orange,
mixed with onyx;
red,
purple,
and yellow.

They call them the spiritual ones.

Butterfly

"I wanna be like them when I grow—
fly high,
be free—
but how can I?"

One of my first mysteries in a new life.

I pitter-patter along,
feeling hungry from excitement,
and searching for green,
rich leaves to munch on—
finding one as rain begins to fall.
Winds pick up,
then greenery disappears.

Butterfly

Feeling nauseous at a noxious breath
as everything turns to gray,
I wonder what happened to the day,
watching animals disappear;

then,
noticing some hunt for prey:

"Gotta find shelter by the end of day!"

Wet and muddy,
ambulating slowly,
I hide beneath a leaf,
where raindrops fall,
mirroring caterpillar reflection
for the first time.

<u>The Caterpillar</u>

Sitting under a dampened leaf—
dew drops dripping down,
reflecting on a young me—
feelings of misunderstanding
misconstrue within,
altering thoughts of purpose:
having no compass in life,
being stagnant,
alone,
in a world full of butterflies
beating vibrant wings,
and soaring over walls,
through open windows
and doors.

Butterfly

Now:
Reflected,
under polka-dotted leaf,
wet,
in soil—

"Who am I?"

I try to foil plans to become and be,
but vegetation cannot protect
caterpillar dreams:
Prey hunt for nutrients in animal decay.

Butterfly

I need to go but I wanna stay
wrapped up in my cocoon,
hidden away,
anticipating—
one day—
that I can fly in sunlit rays,
and wishing I was one of them:
free having purpose,
a direction with no judgement,
just living in salinity
like water petals that bloom.

Soon,
a day will come,
but patience has to be.

The ecosystem is unfair in that way.

The Cocoon

Swathing myself in a butterfly blanket,
hibernating from humanity —
no absorbance to negativity;
just thoughts of yesterday's sensitivity —
pouting,
abandoned in darkness with Keyser Söze,
thinking —
creating an unusual suspect
while an ebbing stance stops in believing
there's no such thing as tomorrow —
no sunshine in this,
no trust in this.

Dead or alive,
what am I in this?

Butterfly

The alternative me wants to be—
conceive—
positivity;
but what's missed
from larva to caterpillar?
No change.
Why can't I be like the others:
flying,
seeing worldly colors,
basking
in rays that canvas blue-tipped wings
flitting in unison to universal song?

Butterfly

For now my cocoon is dark,

with a hint of light from window slits;

raindrops splatter silky bulwark;

soothing noises ease the bane while singing,

"Hello, Darkness.

I don't want to be in you anymore—

don't want these walls closing in anymore.

Darkness,

my friend,

please leave forevermore."

Butterfly

The Pupa stage
isn't what it's cracked up to be:
trying to gain knowledge of oneself—
wanting to move on to the next—
but can't until understanding is outright.
I better get comfy;
the in-between life takes Time
to complete.

With that on my side til then,
I sleep.

Rebirth: Triple 6

Mark of the Beast:
The aspect in nature,
of past theological lyricists,
casting shadows in false nomenclature.

Triple six creates celestial beings —
Atoms in Adam,
winds in Eve.
It makes a mind not believe,
only detecting evil deeds,
existing in the shadow of a living tree
that feeds nonessential seeds:

The Creed,
the Covenant,
amongst Citizens of the Sea of Reed.

Butterfly

Truth:

in false cause—

that keeps vibrations at a low in symmetrical beings—

one cannot escape out of breakable coffer,

shackled in copper sleeves.

The Beast does feast only amongst you:

the west,

the north,

the south and the east.

All believe in demonizing self,

to make one conceive evil within a mean—

Butterfly

since the Fiend lies,

and you are the carrier of the sixes
that make atomic beings.

Pegasus

Recreating a perplexing DNA:
mythical,
like gene editing;
splicing,
then crisping and sequencing
genome reincarnation;
phenotyping,
then characterizing ponderance in existence.

Butterfly

Reshuffling space into theological,
fictional amusement
while a cerebral universe pulsates,
housing a lone helix that collides in anatomical,
Arabian Eve—
sheering away from Adam's atom—
as condiments,
in triple six,
vibrate—
steering headwinds;
detonating,
then showering God's Particle.

A Pegasus spreads its wings,
causing astronomical disturbances,
immersed in constellation configurations.

In a Nutshell

(balling up confiscating lethal injections
misconception imitates reality-insanity
revealing genie-like genius
instantaneous malicious cerebellum
malice and chalice
unreachable serotonin
oxytocin never

Butterfly

long endeavors Iliad Odyssey familiarities
Trojan War similarities hiding com-parities
complimentary sediment twelve cranial nerve
cardiovascular effects no correlation
mutation within abomination pituitary
military installations
sensation numb succumbing rambling of nothing
in a nutshell)

Butterfly Dream

She came to me in a vision within dormancy.

Butterfly

Her wings were platinum,
with an emerald thorax and a lavender abdomen.
Antennas like the evening sun changed colors,
in her affection,
while her milky legs landed near an apricot,
on a mahogany table,
where I sit munching on green Ms:
crunching slowly;
observing,
in amusement—
and some confusement;
brow raised,
cornea to the side,
eyeing a unique creature,
as she inches closer in movement.

Butterfly

Frozen body.

Goose-bumped skin.

No thinking—

just silence within.

She begins to speak.

As parables commence,

leaving no sense

but having a little hence,

riddle me this:

I am Bloom.

I reside in Paris.

I have one wing.

I cannot fly.

I cannot bear to be without the other—

father,

mother—

but none significant.

Who am I?

Butterfly

What am I?

Butterfly

As I stand next to you—
looking in you,
observing one in like—
she speaks of what exactly?
Pondering within past,
present,
future days—
blurring my vision;
reminiscing;
focusing back,
then there she is:

Butterfly

Olive skin;
long,
brownish-blonde hair—
thick and glossy;
her eyes—
almond shaped—
green in color
(Egyptian in origin possibly);
or a Greek from Mount Olympus,
maybe one of the fallen ones,
notably;
lips full,
cheekbones high;
natural in all ways.

Sleepy brown eyes in trance begin to ask,
"Are you for me?"

A question which regards an answer.

Alarm clock rings.

Butterfly

Waking, she disappears.

I want to go back to sleep—

slumber,
till I find her again—

so I begin to count sheep,
hoping,
once again,
I sleep deep.

The Hermit

Being secluded between synapses and neuro-sources,
no one will believe what's in my den
that connects knowledge within,
feeling like the world isn't ready to hear
synoptic topics from Aesop:

Butterfly

Foxes,

ravens,

friends and foes;

philosophical teachings of beings and animals,

linking difference associating the two

in little comprehension;

believing in different dimensions—

butterfly effect,

universal apprehension—

linking one another in Karmic inception.

The snake.

The apple.

Butterfly

Giving commencement mitochondrial Eve—
one mother,
you see—
congruent,
geometrical familial tree:
origination of consummation
leading to tribal manipulation
without genetic desecration.

The Hermit,
secluded:
Manipulating theoretical contemplation,
attempting verbiage in noun-ing assassination;
showing action of isolated toleration to oneself,
succumbing in ponderance,
while others,
who have no tolerance of being in oneself's
constellation—

Egyptian Butterfly

Flying into Amun's arms,
guiding a cinnamon tiger in a buttermilk sky—
sapphire-like—
underneath ancient Thebes,
where the Valley Kings lay with antiquated Queens,
slumbering deep in Osiris' dreams;
where Anubis sits,
weighing the deemed:
scaling ha's and ka's to Ammit in Duat,
akh or not.
All are judged—
some tossed to the crocodile,
hippopotamus and lioness.

Butterfly

The cinnamon butterfly glides,
into temples and homes.
Papyrus lay with scribes,
interpreting sandstone through compound eyes.
As ocelli brighten hieroglyphic lore,
regarding the netherworld and the days of yore,
it reads:

Behemoth geometricians,
erecting trios under the atlas of Sah—
Sirius,
Orion and Lepus—
align Giza to a three-notched belt.

As night melts to day Ra becomes angry,
harnessing strength and power
to a gold-tipped triangle.
It leads to the covenant-conducting reservoirs:
igniting batteries and making electricity.

Thieves strip the Ark.

Energy source depletes.

Butterfly

Bloodbath at the Sea of Reeds.

Butterfly

Locust frogs in darkland;
lambs' blood over doors;
Egypt,
no longer adored.

Shaken to the core,
cinnamon wings glide to the half dog,
to sit upon its flattened nose,
admiring Dead Sea Scrolls,
full of parables from past souls.

The Oracle

"I am Dodona,
the ancient oracle.
I see you've traveled from afar,
pondering if queries could be satisfied,
with compassion that may be intensified,
or cooled down like hoary stars.

Butterfly

Sit my child,

and let us read,

what Delphi's fissure has to conceive,

from a soul that's stressing in self-image,

portraying uncertainty—

uncovered layers without first identified purpose.

Rest quietly my son,

and let the great oracle speak—

in ears that don't want to hear—

ambiguous forthcomings

that will conceive into reality.

Don't worry.

Everything will be ok.

Just understand:

Who you seek in oneself will commandeer,

in future days,

so have no fear."

Butterfly

As Gaia-lucid cavity begins to fracture,
she releases an ominous mist—
thick,
like the morning fog;
hazy,
like a polluted city—
taking breaths away in a vision's blur.
Ate appears,
her cloth—
salmon—
around her neck,
two halves of a crescent
looking away from one another,
attached to a sphere,
with an inverted traverse,
while holding a black butterfly in her left hand,
swaying in Zeus' wind.

Butterfly

Dodona speaks in eloquence,
with sharpness like a scullery knife.
She says,
"This woman is beautiful,
your Athena.
but the Bird of Minerva is not with her.
She speaks in tongues.
Medusa's coating she resides in,
being the yellow dog's apprentice:
Sinister,
but bewildered,
she is wounded like a Harpy,
causing storms within her soul,
cold and desolate.

She is Miseria.

Butterfly

Don't let her venom seep into a doting heart,
turning lighted spirit into darkness.
Keep loving she does not.
Many men—
Odysseus,
Achilles like—
she is the Trojan horse.
She squanders,
yet ponders about your soul.
She wants,
believing in one,
but distance is a must.
She will devour you,
like nymphs singing to sailors
across ocean waves.
Be careful.
Be vigilant.
Be Alpha in diligence."

May

What an interesting day!
She springs.
She blooms.
She brings butterflies out of cocoons—
out of their dooms and glooms.
She brings light,
to guide wings that already exist.

The Butterfly

The day has come!

Courage has fallen on anew.
One foot out of this cocoon,
tasting sunbeam warmth with meter feet:
metamorphosis is finally here,
feeling positive vibrations
in black-tipped wings;
sensing it's a beautiful day.

It's ok;
go play!

Butterfly

Spread wings for the very first time,
flapping them in joy—
such vibrant orange and black.

Now fly:
Go,
soar,
and be.

Taking off,
wend around purple clouds—
like seahorses—
and observe the fiery sunset,
grateful to be alive.

Butterfly

As the sun diminishes,

onyx firmament appears in flickering lantern sky,

to guide away from Gaia's ground,

making this maiden flight so profound—

no sound,

peaceful and heartfelt—

away from meltdowns and dewdrop tears;

no fear,

just joy—

feeling ease,

elated to be with oneness:

something that has been missed...

...now conceived.

Monarch

I believe:

You and me,

better or worse,

death do us part.

Just know:

I've only got fifty-two weeks,

in seven days,

to show my world to you.

Paris

Standing like Eiffel,
her heart the Louver,
triple five makes her symmetrical.
Triple six makes her whole.
Her soul is the Arche de Triomphe.
If she lets you through,
there are twelve cobblestones to get to—
all beautiful,
no darkness or murkiness—
through a dreamy city that never sleeps,
one viaduct above all—
the Jardin De Papillons—
where butterflies stay,
resting on lilies,
dillydallying around:

Butterfly

Some,
caramel in color,
with diamond eyes imprinted on wings;
others with smiley faces,
manifesting Mona Lisa's distinctive smirk
as some pose for spectators—
geometrically—
looking within her soul,
and being stunned in silence.

Honestly she is one of a kind:
always thinking of a way to improvise,
without coded language or hidden figures.
She is exceptional,
methodically.
Meticulous in beauty,
she stands in history.
All places I want to trek through are Paris,
soaking up her soul in sol,
where butterflies roam unrestricted.

Read Between the Lines

Like Van Gogh I gotta cut off an ear
to listen closely,
since Munch's screamer sits at the Café Terrace,
under a starry night,
with the potato eaters,
abstracting in conversation —
switching participles in sentences;
being pro to their nouns;
verb-ing acts with no action —
with uncircumcised sentences,
as a murder pecks at the conscious mind.

Within a Wheat Field of Crows
the living dead reminisce what's missed
in gifting empty words to paramour providers.

The Lily

Resting on a lily,
admiring the light of day,
as a fiery ball sends affection,
warming fonds that frolic and play.

Bear cubs parley
while momma rests in the shade of an oak,
where a sparrow perches,
singing,
"Beautiful day!"

Chipmunks on timber throw nuts
at a woodpecker who knocks—
never stops.

Butterfly

A reckless hare treks through meadows,
golden yellow,
trolling a tortoise whose look,
solemn,
conveys dismay to a journey's end.

As evening ascends,
a lily sundial coats serene woodland grounds,
highlighting an elegant but fragile terrain,
displaying docile creatures—
with shadowy features—
as the Bird of Minerva glides in sun-moon rays,
asking questions;
incarcerating wisdom in sacred days.

Diamond Floe

Cartography misguides a hunter
tiptoeing on a diamond floe,
using suicide blades through Adam's Ale
while Luna's essence reflects,
upon the rill,
her amusement at guiding huntsmen—
like Virgil entertaining Dante—
through nine layers of Hell.

Pausing,
the stalker observes fresh-floured spoors
while the keening cries of wolves echo—
reverberate—
into the black,
and a matte butterfly circles hoar-bitten hands,
pressed to rotten oak.

Black & White Spotted Butterfly

Flitting on an aster—
wings erected at ninety degrees,
still as water,
beautiful as could be,
stunning more than the morning sun—
she sits a whist,
feeding,
mediating her thoughts as I look from a distance,
thinking,

Butterfly

"Who is this mistress—
on this,
a grey and rosy day—
different in all aspects:
black,
with white polka-dots,
golden etches on appendages,
catching ocelli?"
while compound eyes focus on her elegance.

Butterfly

Wings flap quietly,
trying to motion closer:
a pleasant notion to go and talk to her.

Too scared—
can't do it!

First rejection:
what to do if I blew it?

Butterfly

Thank goodness for the fog,
frogs who ribbit,
cottontails that hop,
drowning noises from scales that flap—
hovering in still motion,
admiring her,
believing this butterfly has more to beauty
than most acknowledge.

It's her purity,
gliding back and forth,
pacing,
filtering thoughts proboscis.

Butterfly

I sigh—
heading off,
zooming through foggy day—
as she stops feeding,
and flies away,
dodging into wild,
tall grass;
I hope she didn't notice a drunken butterfly,
misguided in flight.

Perhaps next time,
if I see her again,
I'll give intro
with top hat and cane.

The Night

As the golden sun disappears,
Luna begins to rise:
reflecting her rays—
showcasing glittery,
lavender waves,
crashing onto mahogany sands,
to ignite a matte-black night,
in a frenzied type of way.

As the moon climbs,
the shoreline becomes a party.
Hypnotic music Echoes through obscurity.
Hips begin to sway:
belly dance under way.

Arabian winds sear,
twirling bonfire flames in a narcotic dance.

Butterfly

The chance to see this is rare:

Mind telling eyes to stare,
mesmerized;
nothing to compare the past to this present,
that presents itself—
in a poetic sense—
in Essence.

PART TWO:
THE BOY

The Raven 2.0

Sitting on a rocking chair swinging back and forth,
creaking old cypress pine,
while a grandfather clock strikes twelve,
then stops:
Winds begin to howl,
pushing cracked windows open,
as curtains verve in violence,
shadowing strobed strikes with no rain in sight.
Mind at attention,
picture on a television starts to fade,
while lights begin to dim to an off.
Pupils dilate in darkness:
My autonomic becomes sympathetic.
Dyskinesia-like hands slide on a marble counter,
discovering Lucifer's box—
provoking his red head to strike and flicker:
a bust of Pallas.

Butterfly

Theatrical thinking plays to a questionable mind:
feeling insane like Poe,
but living in modern day with no Lenore,
in a contagion-filled world.
A pelting begins on a dented wooden door.
I open up the flap,
observing bare—
portal shuts to the lair—
sickly shaking fire.
Going back to my chair,
rocking in silence,
disobedient winds keep scowling in defiance,
with blinking lights being noncompliant.
Pelts get louder.
Looking out,
nothing there,
but a sense of something,
somewhere.
Feeling in despair,
sensing something out there—
but where?—

Butterfly

when,
out of nowhere:

A bird.

Butterfly

Nubian in color it sits on the twelve,
gawking;
locking red beady eyes onto mine,
and squawking:

"Nevermore!
You don't adore;
you don't explore.
What is your lore furthermore?"

Butterfly

Sitting quietly,
brow to a raise in dismay,
I have but one reply today.

I must say:

"I do not want to play on this night of day."

Butterfly

"I know nothing of this world —
only transcending through,
picking up lost jewels in bush limbs.
Some hide in the muck and give fuel to life.

Pestilence runs this globe,
driving the sane mad and the mad sane;
and thoughts are just grains of sand,
in the Wadi Rum.

Nevermore!
Nevermore!"
the Raven says.

"Do you not adore the Gods?"

Butterfly

"Only one these days I fear.

His place is either above or below,
but for now the middle must be lived.
Til I die,
I will see gain and loss on Anubis' scale.

Will it lift,
or sink?

Now,
there is something to think."

Butterfly

The raven quotes:

"Your soul is lost.

Your mind dwindles like a spindle,
erasing what was there."

"To be fair,

I do not care.

I have no despair,
and all I can do—
is give caution,
in air."

Butterfly

The Raven quotes again:
"Nevermore,
find Lenore before hair is gray,
wrinkles on skin show.

Pray to your God you score before death,
that the reaper marked on his calendar.
Your soul stirs.

It yearns for love and white doves...

…nevermore!"

Butterfly

Squawking,
"Nevermore find your Lenore,"
it leaves,
and lightning stops.

The trees are still,
the power back:

Butterfly

"Lucifer,"

blown by heated breath.

Wishing

Outside looking into a firefly sky,
wishing—
under the constellation of Cancer—
and hoping for an answer to my emancipation,
while I proclaim simplicity,
in a sleepless night,
consuming a hurt,
burnt blue soul,
so cold in a bitter and sinister midwinter:
wishing for someone to save passion;
feeling matte inside—
unguarded—
my defenses down in senses.

I can't carry feelings that are bare and desolate:

Butterfly

My desert—
quick-sanding skeleton keys—
a frontal-lobe prison with an open door;
oh,
to be freed!

But the fears have been implanted already:
seedling weeds,
to feed a marking Beast.

I wish one day the butterflies will come back,
to subside within.

I really don't want to die inside,
and be eaten alive,
with these salty vibes.

The Masquerade

Ableiten in masking—
seeing who's under who,
without a midnight's toll;
soul searching,
conversing within Dominon's minions.

Anxiety kicking—
cardiovascular in sodium's pressure,
without buoyancy;
then catalyzing enzymes,
aerobically;
systematically mapping in circulatory;
catabolizing dramatic endings in purgatory.

Butterfly

Sending implications through litigation,
unveiling Cleopatra's semblance,
conjuring into Medusa's yellow dog
as a snitcher plays a hypnotizing gizmo,
entangling enchantress in Adam's apple.

The masquerade—
the game:
wondering who's in who,
without a midnight's toll;
sitting in silence,
confiding;
forthcomings combining in eights,
not knowing where the plane begins;
bordering piety and reality,
sending a soul through conformity's end.

Hurting

I'm hurting:
trying to find some peace,
in a mind that's been thinking—
or believing—
that you'll be back someday,
in some way.

A broken heart swings from its hinge,
like the pendulum in a grandfather clock.

Butterfly

I can't sleep:
I keep thinking of you at night,
looking at my watch,
seeing time lapse by without you.

Did you mean what you said,
before you left?

I haven't seen a butterfly in days:
My life I cannot find;
it's somewhere in a diamond maze—
where your voice lay over lilies and asters—
calling my name.

I don't know how to make this better.
I've written you letters but you never answer.

Butterfly

I gasp for air:
with a blank stare I lay,
on a sunny day,
and my heart begins to skip beats.
When you deleted me from existence,
in an instance I became cold inside,
and lost.

What did I do—
What was the cost—

to be sniped in the lungs?

Why?

Why do I feel this way?

Why do I lay in the dark and contemplate my dreams,
that I composite like a conductor:
orchestrating sweet symphonies,
while swinging my golden baton;
lowering oboe and cello,
then raising harps and a piano
that play in a deaf-toned mind?

As the concert ends on a high note,
I envision the crowd's applause,
whistling,
standing,
wanting an encore as I take a bow,
looking to the ground,
with one hand behind my back,
and the other to the side,
suspended in air.

Butterfly

Why is it when I wake up I feel despair,
gasping for clean air—
no baton,
no music;
just thoughts stampeding,
like a crazed fan heading for the stage,
wanting a piece of me,
to be caged and enraged,
hating everything that's seen?

Why is it that this has to be in me?

Never freed when dreams die from spite,
telling Self little white lies,
saying you'll achieve before your demise.

Lying in the matte with punishing thoughts,
saying the crowd is not here for you:
You have no confidence in what you do,
so stop dreaming;
stop believing.

What you're conceiving are dreams that will never
come true due to your overthinking.

The Glass House

Waking in my glass bed,
elevating head from diamond pillow,
and uncovering myself from crystal throw;
then,
sitting up,
planting my feet onto onyx floor,
I look out in observance,
scoping aquamarine—
wooden trees—
as amethyst birds sit and sing,
under a jaded sun that shines high,
across an azure sky,
in springtime.

Butterfly

Bedroom eyes begin to glaze.
They mind an illusional gaze,
at bygones of yesterday—
incarcerating a brain at intervals in age.

Emotions respond like Masons,
laying a fragile foundation—
erecting uneven walls,
with no windows or doors—
for a fabricated abode,
giving an illusion in dilapidation,
so no one can throw stones,
at my internal,
fragile,

Home.

Raw Emotions

Walking through my mind,
Trying to find purity,
but thoughts drown in the blood of swine,
making a soul confined,
in a hole filled with mildew and mold.

As negativity scolds like hot water,
streaming over a blackened-bruised body,
in a world where people sell souls—
make pacts—
with the devil,
to get on different levels,

I've got nothing to hold—
just me in a hole,
trying to fill the mold in an absent role.

Butterfly

I close my eyes,
imagining sunshine rainbows,

and a butterfly;

it flies into a midnight sun-sky,
but the only thing I see is defeat.

My mind is in a dark place;
I cannot call it home:
a glass house made of stone.
There is no door to leave,
and chase my dreams,
in a cold,
damp world.

As sand rains down,
flooding into my abyss—
drowning me;
becoming breathless—
thinking becomes endless,
and right now I feel defenseless,
my mind and body inconsistent.

Butterfly

These emotions are too raw.

I sit and sob,
wondering what went wrong.

Where did I lose control?

Lost

I'm losing my mind,
walking around in a labyrinth and maze,
looking for a way to get out of my conscience.

While staring through a stained windowpane
from an Escher staircase,
observing in obscurity—
watching bisected butterflies sit on divided lilies,
overlooking black,
sandy beaches with broken rubies,
reflecting shattered suns,
signifying a broken soul with desolate feelings;
meeting emotional waves that come and go,
rising and then falling,
with a full moon controlling my liquids,
icing or frying—

I begin to think:
"Existence isn't pleasurable:
not capable to be.

Just conceived to live,
and not understand in being."

Black Cancer

The Dark Side of the Force:
stronger than gravity;
darker than any night,
where no butterfly resides —

just destruction and mutilation within.

Nothing can be sent or received,
making friendship null and void.
The ploy to toil and harbor reaps in seclusion, within
a dark shell.

Butterfly

The Black Cancer never sees the light.
It only feeds on negativity—
destructing,
then analyzing to the Eighth Degree—
believing nothing else matters:
unforgiven,
in a hollow tomb with Hydra's emotions.

Butterfly

All heads battle at the same time,
no matter the carnage or damage to one's soul.

Butterfly

Evil deeds feed the malice seed—
incarnate killer cells invading helper Ts—
to metastasize,
actualize:

Butterfly

Black Cancer.

I'm Giving My All

What can be said when you give your all?
No response when you call—
just an echo through empty halls.

When talking to you—
seeing into your soul—
I can scry you clearly,
being distant,
not knowing what to do;

giving the sun the moon,
and Everything between.

All that has been done is for nothing.

Butterfly

What can I do—
What can I say—
never knowing if it's good enough?

I mean:
What do I have to do to keep you around,
when times are rough?

Please understand:
I'm giving my all to have you—
to spend my life with you;
risking,
in my need;
sacrificing everything in my being;
but believing in me isn't good enough anymore.

Butterfly

You never say the word.
It outweighs every heavy metal on earth:

"Love."

All I can do now is sing your favorite song,
and give my love to have to spend
one more night with you—
to feel your body next to me—
but I can't continue to sing this tune.

Empty halls hear instead the sound—
your name—
called.

Perfect Picture

I painted a perfect picture within my Temple:
hieroglyphs etched throughout—
nothing negative or sinister—
to hold my imagination in contemplation.

Everything in order:
encyclopedic references—
alphabetical,
A to Z—
of existence;
catalogs all in place,
and spaced throughout consciousness.

Butterfly

In the Library of Existence,
leaving an Other's commencement—
trusting in their future achievement,
their colorful vision,
while thumbing through catalogs,
rearranging,
then disappearing:

More come in,
more rearranging;
soliciting,
extending their stay;
Playing with past and future days;
hieroglyphs erased,
painted over,
falsifying imagination;
erecting nonexistent emotions.

I never should have let them in.

Now I'm all confused,
trying to piece together my perfect picture now filled
with toxins and chemicals.

Broken Spell

Thinking about our beginning:
hooking me,
reeling me into the only game you knew—
obsessing to your truth in lies,
laying in bed;
staying awake;
tossing and turning,
with shallow breaths from tears that fall,
beneath rosy cheeks,
onto sateen sheets,
where you once were laid.

Butterfly

Now I'm alone —
looking at the phone,
dialing your number,
hanging up,
trying again —
and thinking I wanna hear your voice,
but all I get is a dial tone,
echoing in empty halls,
leaving a soul at the crossroads,
to love you again,
or to walk away from a sinful spell,
causing my heart to ache —
hoping one day this spell will break,
so I can breathe again,
with tears that fade away.

One day.

Contagion

Viral compatibility:
The inability to break down;
simplicity,
within distancing.

Sociably available to the masses:
confiscating an unnatural disease
that desensitizes sensitivity,
but none do anything to contain.

Butterfly

Low-vibe feelings,
infecting IGs with still photos in motion:
boasting their reality;
silencing insanity in familial trees;
deceiving social circles as this contagion circulates;
toxifying vessels in mind;
blurring occipital lobe;
paralyzing medulla oblongata,
leading to shortness of breath;
tightening the chest,
causing palpitations —
and complex complications.

Quarantine self;
then,
alternating days,
infect the population —
walking around with head down,
head ache.

Butterfly

Belief in victimization will compel an audience
to watch from a distance,
and "love" in an instant.

Depression is the jest—
a fog of mind.
Some understand,
wanting to assist.

Others give up,
and disappear in the mist.

Conviction

You want conviction?
You got it.

Searching deep in my psyche,
summoning consonants and vowels;
then,
manipulating syllables into sentences,
blending synonyms in potential homonyms:

metaphorically speaking,
"Wordsmithin'."

Butterfly

Believing abstract feelings will tell
how homicidal pronunciation
eradicates cerebral thinking,
while conscious verbs reverberate unconsciously,
freeing positive compatibility —
doing away with mutilation of negativity.

Now:

Do you see conviction?
Do you feel conviction?
Do you hear conviction,
articulating from a soul's expression —
emasculating vocabulary
in illustration?

Heavy Heart

Not sure where to start with this heavy heart.
It weighs like an anvil,
dragging a soul down—
making diving faces,
pulling smiles into frowns.
I just want to lay down and not get back up again,
no care about the day;
eyes to close and see no sunshine,
no butterflies,
or birds that sigh.

How do I begin to alleviate the pain?

I've got no one to talk to.
Everybody seems confused—
in their own little world,
battered and used.

Butterfly

I imagine a hearse:
no driver,
no burial,
no Chorus or verse —
no one to lay me down to sleep.

Just me:
six feet deep and naked to the elements,
in earthly sediments.

My mind is hooked on this illusion,
living in confinement of a heart;
it doesn't correlate with the soul —
nothing in my body aligns.

I guess butterflies live alone,
with no companion,
and fly high just to be distracted
from their grief and demise.

Hide-and-Go-Seek

If I could describe you in months,
mid-July would be it:
hot in all aspects —
from mind,
body,
and soul —
that showed life,
like a butterfly that flew freely,
in a dense afternoon.
As we had fun-filled days,
making memories in a summer's blaze,
time motivated our fate,
recollecting our first night date
by arranging constellations —
shaping lamps into hearts,
conveying our love into silence.

Butterfly

Reflected in dilated pupils,
with spite mixed in spate:
Butterfly effect,
happening in the same place;
occurring in different times.

Crazy how the stars align;
then,
one day,
in an instant:
she became distant,
disappearing with no footprints.
Liquid Sunshine removed all trace of
fond memory—
backtracking to her soul—
where she had contentment in yore,
with the Hiram Key in hold.

Butterfly

Now storms rock me mentally,
constantly flooding my mind—
eroding my heart;
shortening electrical systems;
I believe this soul is a walking disaster,
with no FEMA in assistance.

Johnny Blaze

Ghostwriter to your writer:
flaming up synonyms;
antagonizing antonyms to your homonyms;
enforcing homophones to your whether or weather;
living in the present or present.

Yes:
I went there,
their and they're,
confiscating,
then complicating,
vocabulary—
which is kind of scary.

Butterfly

Sitting down for a solo's murdrum,
slicing sentences to a red minim,
resurrecting vowels and consonants to a conundrum,
and giving the masses a palindromes' aibohphobia,
which initiates the headlines,
saying,

"Wanted:
the Sagas of Johnny Blaze,"

is defied on another level of craze—
always on the radar with a rotavator,
tilling complex paragraphs down to simple sentences.

Butterfly of Sorrow

I am crying your tears,
dying from the night before in joy and disaster.

Just the other day I had so much to do,
but I stopped to listen to you.

I should have walked away,
but I couldn't leave you in that way.
What am I suppose to do?
Abandon a shattered heart,
then step on sharp pieces,
tearing my soul to incompletion?

Did I disappoint my future by staying to help?

Butterfly

Am I the butterfly of sorrow,
with wings wrapped around self,
comforting a soul
that wanted to share the wealth?

A Thousand Kisses

If I could give you a thousand kisses:

I would kiss you deep in your soul,
where the hurt and pain resides.

I would pinpoint unhealed wounds
in need of affection,
and seal them with adhesive busses,
hoping the thousand pieces of your heart will mend.

Butterfly

If I could give you a thousand kisses:

I would touch you tenderly,
hoping to erase memories of anguish and hate
that make you contemplate what is true,
and what is illusion,
in your confused world.

I would do so just to see you smile,
(It's been missing for awhile.)
and caress you delicately,
showing love in a butterfly story.

Butterfly

So,
I put your glee on a milk carton.

I hope it will be found one day,
without expiration,
and give you hope again.

But do you really want to find it?

Butterfly

I am just one person
that wants to watch you bloom again.

Bring Your Love

Bring your love.
Maybe I'll bring the shame—
giving you all I've got,
emptying my heart,
draining all of me from existence.

While watching you dance with the devil,
with a dip and a twirl around Medusa's hotel,
I stand at the entrance,
looking back at the trail of love,
then tracing it back to stoned windows and doors
while cobras start to sway:
hissing with split tongues;
flapping their gums;
sensing purity,
while guarding evil.

You Gave Me

You gave me your other wing,
saying:

"Let's hold hands,
and fly away together."

You made me believe in everything:
from breathing,
to a heart recharging and beating
while boosting a mind to a natural high.

Endorphins—
dopamine and serotonin—
drown negative thinking with loving feelings
as blood begins to circulate,
exchanging carbon to oxygen systematically.

Butterfly

I am born again without the Cross,
the Crescent,
or the Star.
By far,
time is tolerable:
Dreams in REM—
reminisced—
like a crisp morning in December,
with logs in a chimney flaring with ember.

Missing those days,
now memories can be remembered.

If I Died Tomorrow

If I died tomorrow,
how would you feel?
Would you still see butterflies fly,
across lavender skies?
Or caterpillars,
twirling silk;
making new homes?

If I died tomorrow,
what would your thinking be?
Would you ponder good times,
believing I'm still around,
while a breath of air makes a cool breeze
that plays with your hair and touches your skin?

Butterfly

Would you smile—
hoping it's me,
and without dismay—
on that beautiful day?

If I died tomorrow,
what would you say at my headstone?
Would you lay flowers—
like a lily,
or an aster—
saying,
"I love you,"
telling me your worries,
dropping heart-shaped tears on my grave?

Butterfly

If I died tomorrow,
how would you know?
Would a butterfly rest on your ring finger,
with one wing showing a sign
that I went to the other side?

If I died tomorrow,
I want you to know:
I love you.
And,
hopefully,
all your dreams will come true.

Because I'll be your spirit guide,
showing you ways to get to—

Silence:

Best
weapon
ever
known
to
man.

Evil Twin

I met you in a place most don't want to go:
Deep in a dark abyss where air constricts,
needing eight Os;
catching malevolent breaths of yours,
from El Diablo's hold.
As I'm trekking through dark,
deep holes —
seeing ember flames igniting in hellish winds,
lighting the way to the River Styx —
while hearing your voice resonating
in a lonely mind —
saying,

Butterfly

"Come find me.

Love me.

Be with me.

Help me.

Follow this articulate tone,

and you will find a beautiful soul." —

I trail Aphrodite's voice in Hades' domain.

Butterfly

Now:

Standing on the banks of the netherworld—

gazing at asphyxiated bodies lurching

under a petrified heart;

seeing arbor thorns stenosing aortic branches,

stemming from a pulmonary trunk—

as Poe's ravens sit on subclavian limbs,

gawking and then talking—

squawking,

"She does not love anymore!

No more!

No love,

forevermore!"—

the heart gently weeps when I see your true self,

perplexed but convinced.

This is who you are:

The evil twin that fooled a soul
into loving an illusional being.

Butterfly Confessions

I must confess in this stress:
Compound eyes have not been focused.
Thinking has been mudded by strutting too much,
and giving too much—
giving more than I should.

But:

If you only had fifty-two weeks to live,
what would you do?
Would you keep all the jewels,
or act like the mule?
give your worth to one who gave you fuel?

The clues were left but never picked up—
only gaffed at and abused.

Butterfly

So,
I must confess:
I did it out of love never reciprocated,
and lacking in understanding—
a butterfly that gave one wing away,
so she could fly away with me...

But she did never—
only using it,
instead,
to elude the one that loved her.

I Love You

I remember the first time you walked into my life.
Thoughts were racing.
I imagined you as my wife—
being faithful in times of strife;
then,
our stories begin.

You catered my thoughts—
my hidden Muse—
and started to rearrange dark-minded days,
that drained my veins,
and rescued my soul from a quicksand hold.

That's when I knew you loved me—
had my back,
like a sweaty tee shirt stuck to an athlete's body,
on a hot summer day.

Butterfly

As we sweated our cupidity,
passion was made,
fireworks displayed,
while listening to Lindita's Cold World.

That turned to a warm desire from your hold.

Finally,
I met the perfect girl.
You understood my moods,
like phases of the moon,
which meant everything to me.

Thank you so much.
You made me believe.
You made me see what existence really means.
I love you,
I really do.

You mean the world to me,

Butterfly

Poetry.

Butterfly

Please,
join this Odist in holy matrimony.

Weapons That Kill

Hate.
Self-destruction.
Mutilation.
Hesitation.
Over contemplation.
Litigation.
Condemnation.

Finding a correlation.

Weapons that kill,
fired from the mind's windowsill;
looking down on everything;
emotions on display in a negative way.

They assassinate your Soul,
setting self up slowly,
to die an agonizing death,
lonely.

You've got to love yourself.

Believe in yourself.

What you have within is a temple of wealth.

Butterfly

Understand the thing at hand:

Negativity breeds negativity;
scrutiny brings mutiny—
a battle between mind and heart.

Weapons that kill make your inner demons strong,
and gleeful in thrill.

Believe in yourself,
loving yourself—
cliché—
or no one else will.

PART THREE:
THE BUTTERFLY

Beautiful Disaster

Existing in a beautiful disaster—
sunshine in one hemisphere—
where butterflies glide,
side by side,
enjoying translucent rainbows that endlessly bend,
searching for their pot of gold

Kids giggle through azure day,
playing tag;
duck duck goose;
throwing some rocks;
competing in hopscotch,
against their two o'clock shadows.

Butterfly

Birds fly high,
chirping—
telling me how they feel,
in a Nina Simone type of way,
as I lay on plush grass,
looking up at origami clouds,
enjoying my stay—

in this beautiful part of my left frontal cortex.

The right is more complex:
disastrous,
malicious to oneself—
dead trees with no leaves,
no children who compete,
no one to sit and eat with me—
and kneading knowledge,
making me make believe.

Butterfly

Now,
feeling alone in a frigid world,
with only death and destruction explored—
gray days with lightning,
igniting my sodium levels,
as I walk alone.

My mind is such a beautiful disaster,
where I walk the line,
as both sides never touch;
but,
stroboscopic light strikes—
rainbows,
igniting topaz,
and milk-like clouds,
making my beautiful disaster not so disastrous.

Beautiful Day

Alighted on an opened window,
a cool breeze brushes stubborn bristles
as I watch an oak tree sway and lean—
a dance and a day bright and warm.
In the newfound,
olive skin wraps a sol's love-giving breath.

Butterfly

Looking around,
then seeing children play—
yelling,
carrying on,
hollering,
(a car horn),
and collecting up hockey sticks off asphalt;
then,
resuming their game as a vehicle passes by—

I fly away to skim the land in poetic fashion:
pausing for a moment to admire the mountains,
the lakes,
painted by the Designer's brush,
and feeling inspiration to write my own creation
from my own five sensations.

I Wrote You

sitting on a park bench,
eating Terry's chocolate,
enjoying the night under Luna's rays—
mixing in a lantern sky
that glimmers off a glassy lake,
as a cool,
crisp breeze starts whipping through hair,
brown and stubborn—
while listening to Sade.

Butterfly

I cherish the day
as my butterfly pen
begins to dance on caterpillar paper:

"My Love,
you're the number eight on its side—
Infinite,
like space,
vast,
and wide."

Sade speaks to me in volumes;
blaring in my ears,
bending eardrums:

Butterfly

Her voice—
angelic,
like yours—
saying,
"You showed me how love can be."
Feeling those words,
with all my soul,
gives confidence and hope once again
to a still born life.

Wishing you were mine,
I would cherish the way
that you and I could hold hands,
on a sol type of day,
tunneling our feet in white,
sandy beaches.

Butterfly

While writing this,
I imagine your emerald eyes
smiling into mine—
your warmth hugging me,
producing endless breaths effortlessly—
and try to paint a perfect picture,
with Dali's surreal vision.
I hope one day you'll read this,
so you can reach out and touch me.

I can keep going,
but this letter would be endless.

So:

I'm going to stop,
and let you breathe it in.

Butterfly

Fifty-Two Weeks

Here I am:
Sitting on an aster,
Reflecting within—
going through my fifty-two weeks,
day by day.

I must say,
I never thought I would come this far—
from learning,
when young,
who to trust,
in my caterpillar phase,
and how to survive in this worldly maze.

Then,
I went to a dark place.
I didn't want to be young anymore.
I wanted to grow and fly away,
never to be found again.

Butterfly

I wrapped myself in a cocoon,
insulated self,
and had daunting thoughts of strife and struggle.
I had no idea who I was at that point—
only acknowledged that the darkness was my friend.

I just wanted the torment to end.
and for this soul to see the sunshine again,
But the fight was on within:
emotions raged,
like a hungry lion in a four-by-four cage.

After awhile,
the storm settled and I felt better,
but I didn't know I had transformed into a butterfly,
and could fly,
be happy,
again.
I found good friends along the way;
who helped me believe the struggle was temporary.

Butterfly

Life is scary,
but you must bury your fears—

and live like it's your fifty-two weeks' end.

May 7 1998

A day that will last in my mind for eternity—
until the Olympic flame is extinguished

from Mount Olympus.

I remember it like yesterday.

So cliché.

But so true.

I was excited for the weekend,
but that day my week ended.

Along with hers.

Butterfly

That was confirmed as my soul stirred,
hoping someone made a mistake —
fake news possibly.

Friday May seventh:
a week before Mother's Day.
I got the news while walking home from school,
carrying my backpack,
on an afternoon hot and sunny.
A breeze glided through thick curly hair,
shook palm trees,
making the day look so peaceful,
but violent.

That was the worst day of my life.

My wife,
my friend,
my mother was gone.

Her voice in my head:
saying my name while I slept.

Butterfly

As I woke up weeping,
but still in a bad dream,
walking around to the sound of nothing, everything
stopped.

I didn't care about friends or the world,
because May seventh was the day my mom left,

and never came back.

Yellow Butterfly

Spiritual in being,
believing when seen,
affirming that she is near:

A yellow butterfly,
flying around;
checking on the living;
saying "Hi" and "I'm alright."

When I think of her through my darkest,
and toughest times,
she floats about;
hovers in the distance,
showing her beauty as observer follows her,
over lush green grass,
as she dances around a tall oak,
leaning in the wind,
where squirrels squirrel around.

Butterfly

But my focus is on this yellow butterfly.
She wants to just say,

"Hi."

As she nears,
resting on warm concrete,
next to my feet,
I watch her,
smiling.

"I know it's you.

Thanks for stopping by.

I love you so much.

I miss you a lot,

Butterfly

Mom.

Butterfly

One day,
I will see you again,
but just know that I'm okay.
As the days pass by,
I've healed to a point,
carrying on,
dropping my baggage,
and leaving it there,
trying not to look back,
and keep moving forward.

Thank you,
Mom,
for flying by.
It means a lot to me in this warm,
frostbitten world,
but as long as I know you're still around...

I'm okay.

Butterfly

I love you.

Butterfly

I should have said those words,
when you were alive.

But I only said them after you died.

Butterfly

Shame on me,
who couldn't speak those words into action,
when you were living.

That's the only guilt I have.

But then,
I was only fifteen you see:
A cool kid;
a hellion in rebellion.

I should've heeded your warnings—
should have just listened to you—
but I didn't.

Is that why you left?

Butterfly

Well,

I see you flapping your wings.

I know you want to leave.

Until next time,
thank you,
for coming by to say hi.

Sorry for being a bad son.

I love you,
Mom."

Butterfly

She rises up—
hovers—
to my nose,
and then flies away.

I guess all is forgiven.

"I hope to see you again one day."

NADER QAMHIYEH
BUTTERFLY

Nader Qamhiyeh is an Arab American poet and lyricist. He lives in Atlanta.

9 781984 584